FREEDOM FROM IMAGINATION

WORDS OF
SHRI NISARGADATTA MAHĀRĀJ

A rendering by
PRASANNA

Copyright © 2014 by Neti Neti Media
Published in United States of America by Neti Neti Media
First Edition 2014 (250 copies)

These quotations are not a literal translation.

Shri Nisargadatta Mahārāj spoke in the Marāthi language. This is an attempt to render in English the essence of what his words are pointing to.

❖

The
"consciousness – I am" is
unimagined imagination.

Everything else is just imagined.

❖

❖

I talk in words
about that which I don't know.

What I know,
cannot be said in words.

❖

❖

This little itch that has come,
the "consciousness – I am" is Brahman.

When the itch goes,
what abides is Parabrahman.

❖

❖

I have seen Sachchidānanda
totally open and butt naked. That
is why my language is like this.

❖

Here, one human being is not
giving knowledge to another human being.

Here, Parabrahman is talking
to the "confused" Brahman.

Identity limited to the body
is the confusion.

❖

❖

No identity remains for ever.
Know this clearly and be free.

❖

In front, in back, up and down,
all around, the space surrounds the body.
That is not the case with the "consciousness – I am." Because the light of that
consciousness itself means space.
After the limited identity with the body goes, you yourself will know
the all-pervasiveness of your own "Being."

❖

When you can really say: "I don't know",
then you will be the Supreme – Parabrahman.

❖

There is ignorance as long as
there is knowledge.

❖

❖

What is the primary imagination?
It is this – "I amness". The touch you have
of the "consciousness of your beingness."
That is the primary dream.

The "unimaginable" has imagined: "oh, yes – I am."
This dream of "I amness" is only for a blink of an eye.

❖

A pinprick of "knowingness" has flashed against
the background of my innate "not-knowingness".
In it appear all the universes.

There is no movement in that which is aware of "knowingness."
It abides ever unchanging.

❖

All this is like a sleeping man
witnessing a dream.

❖

❖

The "consciousness – I am"
is unimagined imagination.
Everything else is just imagined.

❖

Did you ever imagine that some day you will know that you are?

Whatever can be known is only imagination.
Whatever is known is not "Self-Knowledge."

What is the primary imagination?
It is that "we are." That "we are awake."

In absence of this imagination, what can we say about ourself?
Right now you are. Even without the imagination, you are.

❖

"Self" is free from the imagination that it should be.
That is why there is no further freedom for it.

❖

❖

"I" just dreamed a dream of "I amness."

Whatever is in absence of that dream is not anything or anybody.

❖

That which is known knowingly is changeful.

"That" which knows unknowingly is changeless.

That which is not everpresent is not Truth.

❖

Actions of the body cannot put any blemish on the formless, changeless, Pure Consciousness.

If you try to paint the sky black,
only your hands get dirty.

❖

❖

That which can say: "I am",
is prior to saying "I am."

This light is brighter than the waking state and it is more hidden than sleep,
because it recognizes deep sleep.

❖

There was no awareness that "I am."

Now there is awareness that "I am."

That is the primary or root-illusion.

❖

The "consciousness – I am" is transient. That which knows it is eternal.
In search of the Eternal Truth, how can dependence on the transient be of any help?

Hold on to the Awareness that is present
regardless of being aware of something else or not.

❖

❖

The "consciousness – I am" itself is seen as the vision of the world.
This is our direct experience.

❖

Dream is seen within but it seems to be outside. Similarly, the waking world
is seen within, but it seems to be outside.

❖

Even if you don't do anything, the appearance of the world is not going to stop.
Is it possible to cremate this movement from sleep to waking
and from waking to sleep?

❖

It is our "sense of being alive" – that is shining as all this. The real seeker will know this
clearly.

❖

❖

The dream world means incarnation of the mind. Similarly,
the waking world is also incarnation of the mind.

❖

The "knowledge – I am" is worldly. Beyond it is total fullness.

❖

What is "seen", flows from us.

❖

First the consciousness of our being – "I am." Then without any material
the world is born from it, as it does in a dream.

❖

Mind cannot know what is beyond the mind. But, what is beyond the mind
knows the mind.

❖

❖

You don't disappear in time.
Time disappears in you.

❖

You do know what is beyond time, very clearly and absolutely. You are not aware of it because you have no time for discerning it.

Eternal has neither remembering nor forgetting.
Your "Being" cannot be measured in time.

See it as it is. Don't imagine.
Don't become anything, you will be trapped again.

❖

That because of which everything is known or seen is not known or seen.
Even though IT IS.

❖

❖

The "Self" by itself is unimagined.

The "Unimagined-One" is revealed after knowing the imagination as just imagination.
After knowing the nature of imagination, you will know that this world is just a joke.
Nothing has happened, nothing has gone.
I have not seen anybody, nobody has seen me.

Mind itself is imagination and imagination itself is the mind.
Imagination gives birth to whatever it likes.

❖

You don't know this because you have become the disciple of your mind.

❖

❖

In my innate nature there is no sense of "Self."

❖

There is sweetness in sugar, saltiness in ocean.
In this body there is love – the sweetness of knowing "I am."

Live in the present moment. Why?
Because the present moment is the "touch" of your being.

❖

Tell me, what is the lifespan of a moment?

❖

Now we know that we are. That which is aware of this knowledge should be known.
Then everything will be known.

❖

❖

My birth is not true. It is imposed on me unknowingly.
How can I believe it to be true?

It is not possible for anyone else to see your dream except you.
Similarly, your waking world is for yourself only.

❖

The "knowingness" disappears after knowing it for what it is – a dream, an illusion.
What abides after that has no name.

Experience can be described in any number of ways.
But the experiencer cannot be described.

❖

The richness I have without the company of "knowingness" is beyond words.

❖

❖

Can the Sun ever see darkness?
Can the Sun ever find the end of its own light?

Your consciousness is not some itsy bitsy thing.
The whole universe means the radiance of your consciousness.

But you are not that. You are the "knower" of that.

❖

Is there duality between the consciousness and that which is aware of it?
It is just like the duality between the Sun and its light.

Manifest - consciousness itself is the "other".
Unmanifest - "none-other."

❖

❖

Remember ......

In this corpselike body of yours there is a seed
full of light of the Supreme.

Pay attention to that light.

On recognizing it, its infinite nature will be revealed.
The word human applies to the body, not to the "Self."

How can that whose nature is light be the body?

❖

You are the "Light" that reveals - both the light and the darkness,
the knowledge and the ignorance.

❖

Transcend the body even while it is experienced.

❖

❖

This light of "knowingness of beingness" is the image of the Supreme.
News of your own beingness is the announcement of the Absolute.

❖

Hold on to that which you "know" before knowing anything.

❖

Forget what people say. Look, what is your form for yourself?
Only you are.

Formless.

❖

Have you ever thought about your own light?
Light you see outside shines in your light.

You say you can't see your own light. How can the source of seeing be seen?

❖

I have nothing to do with this talking. It is just like the sparrows chirping.

❖

Your "livingness" is alive even without your knowing that you are.
This is not recognized because of your knowing that you are.

❖

❖

Is it a small matter that you know that you are?
Isn't it the truth that only you know this?

So make the "knowledge of your being" and your "Being" into one
and see what miracle happens.

The "Ultimate Realization" is that simple.

❖

If you really are, keep looking at yourself only.

❖

It is the "Ultimate" where the consciousness or "knowingness" dissolves.
It is not bound by time.

❖

When you will see your "Self" you will find it even more empty than a dream
– fully, totally empty.

❖

❖

The "knowledge of your being" has no color, no form. But it has a "taste"
– the taste of the "memory of being".

Truth has no taste, which means it is without the "knowledge of its own being."

❖

With your attention landing on your "Self" even for a moment, you will find that
you are freedom itself.

❖

Where there is no "knowledge of being", what else is there?

❖

❖

Do sleep and waking happen because of the cleverness of your intellect?
Or do they happen spontaneously?
Think about that.

Whatever you are not, let it come to naught.

❖

Words have to be used to talk about the "Reality" beyond the words.

❖

Now – you are.
Your life's activities go on based on imagination.

Even without imagination – you are.

❖

❖

What is the primary illusion?

"I amness."

Yes, the illusion is there, but remember, you are the "knower" of that illusion.

❖

What is lit is burning.
What is burning is shining.

❖

One who knows that the "knowingness of beingness" arises and subsides
is free.

One who believes that everything known by that "knowingness" is real,
is bound.

❖

❖

In the realm of Non-Duality, no other proof can be found, nor any imagination.
You are your own proof.

That which is Non-Dual, that which is complete and full
has no separate experience of bliss, nor can it be witnessed.

The "consciousness – I am" is spontaneous.
It is not imagined by anyone.

❖

You already know your true nature,
but you have not taken delivery of that knowledge.

Your money order has arrived, but you have not cashed it.

❖

❖

Ultimately, what is the essence of all this seeking?
It is to find out what this "sense of being alive" really means.

In dream it feels like you did all kinds of things. But actually did anyone do anything?

❖

Can "seen" be there if there is no "seer"?

❖

The seer of the dream sees the whole world in it.
Has anyone from that world seen the seer?

A dream arises in sleep and goes back to sleep.

You are just a witness from a great distance.

❖

❖

How can you remember that which you have never forgotten?

❖

Now you have the news of your being, don't you?
That knowledge was not there is true too, isn't it?

"That" which did not know – knows it now.
If "That" was not present, could this be known?

❖

That which cannot be forgotten is eternally present.

❖

Whatever can be remembered is bound to be forgotten.

❖

❖

To forget is the nature of the mind.

But the "Lord of Consciousness" is ever awake, even during sleep.
World is the name for the waking state itself.

❖

Being "awake" but not experiencing a single word is the Pure Being.

❖

Does the mind know you or do you know the mind?
You are not the mind. You are the "knower" of the mind.

The "knower" cannot be described.

❖

Mind cannot know what is beyond the mind.
But what is beyond the mind knows the mind.

❖

❖

The meaning of what can be called the root-thought is just "Yes".
That has no form.

-------Only the space lighted up-------

You are empty like space.

You are neither small, nor big. Like space you are unbroken and solid,
without any hole or crack in it.

❖

Your presence pervades all emptiness.

The solid mass of Pure Consciousness is named Parabrahman – the total absence of
the illusion "I am" or "I am not".

❖

❖

The memory of a thing you have seen is not that thing.

The memory of my being is not my "Being."

The "consciousness – I am" is not what I am.

❖

Where there is no "consciousness of being" who would say something is or nothing is?

❖

"Self" cannot be an object of knowledge.

"Knower" is not the knowledge of any kind.

❖

❖

Could "that which is not" have the memory of its being,
or "that which is" knows – "I am"?

The appearance of this memory itself is Māyā – the illusion.
That itself is the mother and father of ignorance.

Nature of appearance is to disappear.

You never appear or disappear.

❖

Go back to the point where you never had any experience of any kind.

❖

❖

What is all your talk about miracles?
Is there any greater miracle than the emergence of the experience you have of your own being?

❖

Unmanifest is the Truth.

Manifest is timebound.

❖

I am not what happens. I am that which "IS", but has never happened.
Whatever is known becomes unknown, but that which knows is peaceful.

❖

All trouble is for consciousness only. There is solid peace at the bottom of it.

❖

❖

The Supreme – Paramātmā is so absorbed in himself that
He doesn't even know that "He is".
But this does not mean sleep.

Even there - you are, keeping watch over it.

❖

Who witnesses that sleep was very good and deep?

What is it that wakes up?

Who witnesses the "knowledge of beingness"?

❖

In deep sleep you are pure ignorance. If that ignorance or the sleep does not wake up,
who is born and who dies?

Everyday that ignorance wakes up and goes back to sleep.
Waking state is the child of ignorance.

❖

❖

That which wakes up in the morning has no need to ask anyone:

"Am I awake?"

This is internal knowledge.

❖

When you "realize", there is no need to go around shouting, "I have realized."
People will know.

❖

The feeling that something special has happened to me is the ego.

❖

❖

What is all this?

The need to eat again, to sleep again, to wake up again.

The belly of "becoming" is never filled.

Can this constant itching be the nature of my "Being"?

❖

You say, in meditation the "knower" disappears.

Who knows this?

You say, in meditation the experience comes – "there is nothing."

What is the nature of that which knows – "there is nothing"?

❖

❖

Truly speaking there is no birth, no death. Only what is known ceases to be known.

That is it.

❖

The world is made of your light.

❖

To believe that you are seen in the light of the world is bondage.
It should be realized that the world is seen in your light.

❖

What is there where "I am" not?

❖

❖

Have a firm conviction that I am prior to
whatever is experienced between waking up and going back to sleep.

What does it mean to wake up?

It is the shining of consciousness as the sense "I am."

❖

In this body you are not like the body. But you are Pure Consciousness
reflected in the body as "I – consciousness."

Radiance of that consciousness is the world.

❖

When the Pure Consciousness will come to your attention, you will realize that
you are the boundless ocean of peace.

❖

❖

Now, you feel that you know.

What you know is not you.

You are "That" which knows.

"That" is not some "thing."

But "That" certainly Is.

Really ....

Only "That" is.

❖

The "Knower" is unknowable.

Know what is known and put a stamp on it: "This I am not!"

❖

❖

Everyone is same in deep sleep.

Separation begins with waking up.

❖

"That" which gives you the knowledge of your being is with you, always.
Then why are you wandering here and there?
Can "That" be found in the world out there?

Stop here.

❖

I can tell you to do whatever you like. But you will not be able to digest it.
So I say.....

Tear down the imagination of being a "doer" and then do whatever you like.

❖

❖

The essence of this entire world is "I amness"
or the "sense of being awake."

First the dream-space is projected from you – in you, then a world in it.
You act in that world as some person.

All this happens unknowingly.

Truly speaking nothing has happened.

❖

First, you are.
Then thoughts arise.

If you are not present, to whom can thoughts appear?

❖

❖

Waking that comes in the morning functions the whole day and goes back to sleep.

Someday you will realize.......
Even this waking you are not.
Someday this waking will go back to sleep forever.

Sleep means ignorance.
That ignorance wakes up every morning and goes back to sleep.

❖

What surrounds the "sense of being awake" is the Eternal Truth.

Sleeplike "not-knowing" surrounds the flash of "knowingness".

❖

❖

Is space seen in deep sleep?

What is the dwelling place for space?

Where does space live?

❖

The light of the "sense of being awake" is the space.

❖

The "knowledge of our being" is a seedless sprout - a virgin birth.

❖

How I am before knowing that "I am" should be known.

❖

❖

Your "knowingness" has no shred of imagination in its nature.

It only has "Light."

The Essence of that "Light" means "Isness" or "Yes."

❖

What light do you use for seeing the dream?

When the dream is over, the world is gone. What happened to the witness of the dream?

He never came, he never left.

❖

❖

What is the real essence of the search for the ultimate?

To find out the Truth and the Untruth about ourself.

Whatever can be found is the Untruth.

❖

When the "knowledge I-am" tries to see itself, its "knowingness" disappears.

❖

Pure Consciousness is infinite, boundless. There is no measure to its extent.
How can that have death?

How can sky die?

❖

❖

Don't get caught up in efforts of getting something or giving up something.

Just remain quiet.

It is the mind that is born,
not you.

❖

In ignorance I said:
"I was not."
Here is the catch.......

One who knows "I was not" is saying this!

❖

❖

This wakefulness and sleep are not two. They are "not-two."
One is transformed into another.

Only the "knower of both" knows this.

❖

Don't focus on what is known by consciousness.

Meditate only on the consciousness itself.

❖

The "sense – I am" is imagination. Imagination happens.
How can that be stopped?

Just know, "I am not the imagination" and be free.

Is it necessary to say:
"don't eat the dirt?"

❖

This knowledge is for knowing. Not for licking.

❖

The waking state experience is absent in dream.
The dream state experience is absent in the waking state.
The waking state experience is absent in sleep and the sleep state experience is absent in the waking state.

The experience of "I amness" is present only in two states of waking and dreaming.

Can "That" which knows these experiences to be transient ever be absent?

❖

After knowing the "Self" it will be clear that the "knower" is unborn.

❖

The joy of being free from imagination
is out of this world.

❖

❖

Everyday you leave yourself and go into deep sleep.
Are you going to quarrel with someone if that sleep never wakes up?

❖

Why did you wake up from deep sleep? Why did you go to see a dream while fast asleep?

Can there be an answer to this?

❖

No waking, no world.
Waking itself is the world.

❖

From where and how did this experience of this world and ourself arise?

How we are in absence of this experience should be known.

❖

❖

The "consciousness – I am" means "the knowingness of beingness."

That which is aware of that "knowingness" has not an iota of "knowingness."

❖

I am talking about that "which was not" and "will not be."
Nothing can be said about that which "Is."

❖

This knowingness has come unknowingly. How can you hold on to it knowingly?

❖

This "knowingness" is understood to be the opposite of "not-knowingness."
But without "knowingness", both are not.

❖

❖

You have theories about how this consciousness is created.
But they are invented after this consciousness is present.

What can be said if the consciousness is not present?

This consciousness is neither a man nor a woman, or any other thing.
But everything is because this consciousness is.

❖

You are the "Self-Aware" Light. The whole universe appears within your light.

Self-Awareness is not dependent on thinking.

❖

❖

Scholars and scientists will search for what has happened in all that has happened.

There can be no investigation into what already is but has never happened.

❖

You will be free when you realize that you have never known anything.

Feeling that something is known is just an itch.

❖

Tear down the imagination that there is something called "Ātmā" or "Self" and that there is something called "Paramātmā" or the "Supreme Self."

❖

❖

When did I come to my attention first?

How did I become aware of myself?

Can this be known by reading scriptures?

❖

Nobody can have experience of Truth. Nature of experience is to go away.

Is Truth some character in a play so that it may appear on the stage?

Does Truth need to wear some costume?

❖

That which is aware is far from awareness.

❖

That which is aware is far from awareness.

❖

Consciousness you have today is just the news of your being.
A telegram has arrived saying: "You Are."

❖

While listening to this talk, keep your attention on that which is aware of the feeling:
"I am listening."

❖

❖

Standing on Earth you see the Moon with your eyes.
What is there between the eyes and the Moon?

Space.

Space can't be seen with your eyes.
Similarly your own light – the light with which you see – can't be seen by you.
Because both are only one.

Space is the light of your "sense of being."

❖

What is seen without the eyes is Truth.

❖

❖

The space and myself are not two.
So wherever I go, I will go where I am, already.

But wherever I go with the body-identity, I will go where I am not.

❖

Don't be the buyer of any of your concepts.

Imagined imagination's hunger is never satisfied.

❖

The world appears because of the sense of being awake. They arise simultaneously.

The unknowingly known news of your being is love.
It embraces the whole world.

❖

❖

The "consciousness – I am" is in the body that has a boundary.
But that consciousness has no form – it has no boundary.

The "knowledge – I am" itself is called consciousness.

❖

❖

You say: "I am."

If the word "I" is removed, what can you say about yourself?

No answer. Just "Silence."

This state is prior to the awareness of consciousness.

❖

That which leaves the body and goes, but is never seen coming or going.......

You are That.

❖

Attention removed from other things, returns back to the "Self."

❖

❖

Just sit and keep looking to see what this "I" means.
Don't take advice from the mind.

If the mind is active, let it be. Just make sure to know that you are not the mind.

You say, you are carried away by the mind.
Have you ever seen the "sense – I am" carried away?

❖

Mind will never be under control as long as it knows you in the form of a body.

❖

❖

The manifest consciousness "I am" is the reflection of "what is."

It is not "what is."

❖

Who knows that the mind is peaceful or the mind is restless?

Hold on to that.

That essence sees everything. No one can see that essence.

❖

What is known before knowing anything else?
The "news of your being."

Who knows it?

Can't be said.

❖

❖

What is transient?

The "consciousness – I am" is transient. That which is aware of this is eternal.

How can the transient experience the eternal?

❖

You can't collect this knowledge by sending the goons of your intellect.

❖

Pure Consciousness is everywhere,

but outside the body it does not have the "taste" of its beingness.

❖

❖

What is called our "Self" - that does not come or go.

What is there when the word Self is removed? How can that be described?

❖

On realization of Truth,
the "knowingness of our beingness" will not be known knowingly.

Also it will not be known that it is not known.

❖

To Pure Consciousness, there never was any experience. Nor is there any experience now.

❖

❖

When you can truly say: "I don't know"
then you will be the Supreme, the Ultimate, the Absolute -Parabrahman.

❖

It is enough to know only once, what is Truth and what is Untruth.
Then where is the need to sit in "Samādhi" again and again?

❖

❖

For myself I have no color, no design.

I am the witness of "isness" and the "absence of isness".

❖

When I look beyond the mind, I see the witness.

Beyond the witness, there is infinite intensity of Emptiness and Silence.

❖

What is my attainment? I know that I don't know anything at all.

I have seen plenty of things that have not happened.

❖

I have no teaching. Just listen. I am telling you about "what is" and "how it is."

❖

❖

What is there in the end?

Nothingness......

Not even that.

❖

There is nothing left of me even to say that I am free.

❖

❖

After hearing this you may not want to see my face again.

But if the Truth of what I have said reaches you, you will run from a million miles away and touch my feet.

❖

The joy of being free from imagination is "out of this world."

Made in the USA
Middletown, DE
03 June 2018